Outlaw Style

OUTLAW STYLE

Poems by R. T. Smith

The University of Arkansas Press
Fayetteville
2007

Copyright © 2007 by The University or Arkansas Press

All rights reserved
Manufactured in the United States of America

ISBN-10: 1-55728-853-4
ISBN-13: 978-1-55728-853-0

11   10   09   08   07   5   4   3   2   1

Designed by Liz Lester

⊗ The paper used in this publication meets the minimum
requirements of the American National Standard for Permanence
of Paper for Printed Library Materials Z39.48-1984.

LIBRARY OF CONGRESS CATALOGING-IN-PUBLICATION DATA

Smith, R. T.
Outlaw style : poems / by R.T. Smith.
p.   cm.
ISBN-13: 978-1-55728-853-0 (pbk. : alk. paper)
ISBN-10: 1-55728-853-4 (pbk. : alk. paper)
I. Title.
PS3569.M537914O87   2007
811'.54—dc22
2007023579

for Sarah Kennedy,
sui generis, sine qua non

"He had a dream and it shot him."
—HUCKLEBERRY FINN

CONTENTS

ACKNOWLEDGMENTS

Arts & Letters: "Carrion Cry"; "Strange Fruit, 1939"

Asheville Poetry Review: "The Restless Dead: Walker County, Georgia"

CrossRoads: "Johnny Shines' Last Edict on the Taproot of Delta Blues"

Gettysburg Review: "Hohner"; "Sump"

Georgia Review: "Gypsy Fiddle"; "Summertime"

Green Mountain Review: "Mandolin"

Iron Horse Literary Review: "Site Visit: Ford's Historic Playhouse"; "Brother Fain Carouthers, Summoned"

The Journal: "Thrush Witch"

Missouri Review: "Asia"; "Booth from Beyond"; "Booth Keepsake"

National Poetry Review: "The Sacred Sound of the Dove"

Pleiades: "Shepherd Ollie Strawbridge on the Chicken Business"

Ploughshares: "Dar He"

Poetry: "Outsider Art"

Sewanee Review: "Scuppernongs"; "A Pentecostal Note"

Southern Humanities Review: "Energy"; "Exhuming Booth"; "Charm: Anna Surratt Tonry, 1900"

Southern Poetry Review: "Booth: A Quick History"; "Plantation of the Mad"

Southern Review: "Ebony: John Wilkes Booth Recites 'The Raven'"; "The Prophet Boston Corbett on Shooting Booth"

Verb: "Edwin Booth at the Players' Club: Portrait by John Singer Sargent, 1890"; "One-Man Show"

Several of these poems were published in *Ensemble,* a limited-edition chapbook from Talking River Publications in Lewiston, Idaho.

"Dar He" received the Cohen Award from *Ploughshares* and was reprinted in *Pushcart Prize XXX*. "Plantation of the Mad" received the 2006 Guy Owen Prize from *Southern Poetry Review*.

My sincere thanks to Sarah, Chuck, Natasha, Diann, Claudia and Kent, Kirk, Brendan, my students (especially the *Shenandoah* interns), all the editors who generously granted space to these poems, Enid, John, Bob, Mark and Kimberly, who let me ride Rusty, as well as Hank Dobin and W & L for the time to fine-tune these poems.

Outsider Art

Thrush Witch

When my tongue went white as hen feathers
and the gentian violet failed, mother
sent for Miss Olene in lieu of a doctor.

I could not warble a word, but wept
from the veil of fungus, as she knelt
by my cot on the sleeping porch and felt

my neck and brow. "This child has the thrush,
sure enough," she said. "Hermit bird in the bush
will steal a boy's voice to sweeten its wish

to become the most musical thing. Don't fret.
I won't suffer you to suffer. Now shut
your eyes and see him on the wing." With that,

she touched her mouth to mine. Her breath,
flowing in, rendered a sweetness worth
more than any song I'd ever heard. A thirst

shook me as she sucked out with a rush
and shiver all my pain. Then I could just
hear her whisper, in that raptured voice,

"Fly back to Jordan, bird. Child, you hush."

Brother Fain Carouthers, Summoned

As a boy under Razorback Ridge near Laurel Run
where a wildfire licked the thicket in the fifties,
I would find them in April on sunstones, dozing,
a knot-cluster or a lone satin-back looped over, slack
and harmless as a fire hose, and I would snatch
him up by the rattle end and crack him in cool air
like a muleskinner's whip just to see the arrowed
head explode, just to collect his little bells of bone.

But that was before Brother Summers, who handled
at Dolley Pond, Scrabble Creek, and Jolo, before
word came how hard we needed hot gospel here.
And lo, he wore the crown of snakes on his brow
and the stole of braided living temptation tasting
our heat, and he showed me in Hiram's brush arbor
beside the living water how to walk unafraid
in a copperhead tangle, how to gather diamondbacks
like so many kittens, nor was I frightened, nor struck
while the brothers and sisters from over in Goshen
danced to a scarred Martin guitar and the burning
Word. Hallelujah. We are washed in the blood,
hamona-chozosma. The wicked I have walked among
and fought with and abandoned will call us daredevils
and madmen, but I can read the cursive letters
of a serpent's spine and look him where the wet eye
shines beneath its hood to seek my sweating face.

Even now something is coming to me by lying still
in his mesh box with scripture scarlet on the lid:
They shall speak with new tongues—they shall
take up serpents. The words I utter are of no earthly
tribe, though angels whisper them and the Holy
Ghost listens and urges the sinner in me to sway
that wonders shall perform, Oh, *shanamaniala-roe,*
and he is stirring now, his heart-shaped head
spitting black lightning. The anointing quickens
my blood as the tambourine shivers and the house
shakes like a weave room with its looms roaring.

I have seen the weaver's shuttle in flight when lint
like snow filled the air, and I have heard the strings
humming the hymn of weft and warp until patterns
like fate formed on new tapestry. I have longed
to touch the cotton in motion, but its spell is nothing
to the canebrake's eye, the coontail's braided sull,
the scent of dusty scuppernong leaves, and I no longer
yearn to take up the pool cue, longneck bottle, nor
necklace on a perfumed woman but want only this,
a reason to kneel and gather to my bosom the devil
tamed in the faith, *ohfala-shanta-hava* and the still
waters at Jesus Name Chapel of Servants Learning,
where I can see moonlight through the window
falling on late wheat and the faces of glory angels
as my neighbors shake and pray around me. I know
false prophets will fall away and we will receive
gifts of tender mercies, *rachamin,* and I am praising
the Lord shining and ready to go mouth-to-mouth

with Zion's fierce breath better than any textile
king's paycheck, better than motel sex or the other
old curses, for God has lain on my heart and said
I am in no danger from one whose head is bruised
by my heel, and this room with no pews or pulpit
is the grace garden. I am coming as he calls me,
that stillness stirring his shape to a coil question.
I am anointed, praising his holy fire and the ordeal
of touching living evil, and if his fangs gleam
and if he licks out, if he takes me in my frenzy,
I could not suffer more happily, and if I die
it will mean the Lord Jesus is ready to add my name
to the living scroll, for the message is far deeper
than mortal understanding. It is blaze-blinding
tonight from far beyond with red words swirling
like thread on a bobbin, all shining with use now
and always far sweeter than tongue can tell.

Energy

On days like this, Roosevelt's whirligigs
reap the wild wind. He calls them "lilies."
From cast-offs and scraps he's fashioned a dozen
by sawing silhouettes and welding axles.
They're huge. Two sows he shaped from barn wood

dip round snouts in a purple trough and twirl.
A woodpecker sleeker than any coon hound
snaps his flame head back and forth with every gust.
Animals and sinners, a granny churning—
Roosevelt loves to show them off. On this hill

he's lived long enough to cuss twelve governors,
made his life from firewood, burley, and corn,
smaller whirligigs he hawks at roadside.
A blush-throat hummingbird's propeller wings
sing. Two farmers shear a black sheep's wool,

and over there beside the rows of Fraser
firs he pampers, a man and black bear take turns,
using mallets to drive a peg that never moves.
He calls it "beauty," the way a gale can find
the patient vanes stalled and drive them to circle

in dervish fury, convert what's rushing
past to brightness as limber flanges flash.
Not a church-prone man, he does love praising.

"Have you raised your Ebenezer?" he asks,
as tin angels swivel and a chimp bows

his fiddle. "This," says Roosevelt, "is labor
put to proper use, a field of lilies
in the spell of whoever oversees the air."
Today the chains and gears scream for oil
inside towers that could pass for drilling rigs,

and the breeze announces a storm, but Rose
won't quit adjusting the yellow petals
he's sweated onto copper stems with solder.
"It's my weather garden. It's my meadow,"
he says, "my crop for better-than-cash. A man

in turmoil could come here to unsuffer."
Guy wires tense, as every pawl and pivot
snaps to action. His flowers mill the wind.
They harvest energy to bestow design.
When I ask if this reeling is a righteous fate,

he points to their orderly frenzy and grins.
"My gigs spook the devil back to his den.
They may not toil, but Lordy how they spin."

Dar He

When I am the lone listener to the antiphony of crickets
and the two wild tribes of cicadas and let my mind
wander to its bogs, its sloughs where no endorphins fire,

I will think on occasion how all memory is longing
for the lost energies of innocence, and then one night—
whiskey and the Pleiades, itch from a wasp sting—

I realize it is nearly half a century since that nightmare
in Money, Mississippi, when Emmett Till was dragged
from his uncle Mose Wright's cabin by two strangers

because he might have wolf-whistled at Carolyn Bryant,
a white woman from whom he had bought candy,
or maybe he just whispered "Bye," as the testimony

was confused and jangled by fear. The boy was not local,
and Chicago had taught him minor mischief, but what
he said hardly matters, as he never got to testify,

for the trial was for murder after his remains were dredged
from the Tallahatchie River, his smashed body with one
eye gouged out and a bullet in the brain and lashed

with barbed wire to a cotton gin fan whose vanes
might have to him seemed petals of some metal flower,
had Bobo—as friends called him—ever seen it. And why

this might matter to me tonight is that I was not yet eight
when the news hit and can remember my parents at dinner—
maybe glazed ham, probably hand-whipped potatoes,

iced tea sweeter than candy, as it was high summer—
shaking their heads in passing and saying it was a shame,
but the boy should have been smarter and known never

to step out of his place, especially that far south. Did I
even guess, did I ask how a word or stray note could give birth
to murder? He was fourteen, and on our flickering new TV,

sober anchormen from Atlanta registered their shock,
while we ate our fine dinner and listened to details
from the trial in Sumner, though later everyone learned

the crime occurred in Sunflower County, and snoopy
reporters from up north had also discovered that missing
witnesses—Too Tight Collins among them—could

finger the husband Roy Bryant and his step-brother
named Milam as the men in the truck who asked, "Where
the boy done the talking?" and dragged Emmett Till

into the darkness. His mother Mamie, without whom
it would have all passed in the usual secrecy, requested
an open-casket funeral, so the mourners saw the body

maimed beyond recognition—his uncle had known
the boy only by a signet ring—and *Jet* magazine
then showed photos, working up the general rage

and indignation, so the trial was speedy, five days
with a white jury, which acquitted, the foreman
reporting that the state had not adequately established

the identity of the victim, and I don't know how
my father the cop or his petite wife the den mother
took it all, though in their eighties they have no love

for any race darker than a tanned Caucasian. I need
a revelation to lift me from the misery of remembering,
as I get the stigma of such personal history twisted

into the itch of that wasp sting. Milam later told *Life*
he and Bryant were "guilty as sin," and there is some
relief in knowing their town shunned them and drove

Bryant out of business, but what keeps haunting me—
glass empty, the insect chorus fiercer, more shrill—
is the drama played out in my mind like a scene

from some reverse *To Kill a Mockingbird*—or worse,
a courtroom fiasco from a Faulkner novel—when
the prosecutor asked Mr. Wright if he could find

in the room the intruder who snatched his nephew
out of bed that night, and the old man—a great uncle,
really—fought back his sobs and pointed at the accused,

his finger like a pistol aimed for the heart. "Dar he,"
he said, and the syllables yet echo into this raw night
like a poem that won't be silenced, like the choir

of seventeen-year insects, their voices riddling strange
as sleigh bells through the summer air, the horrors
of injustice still simmering, and I now wonder what

that innocence I miss might have been made of—
smoke? rhinestones? gravied potatoes followed
by yellow cake and milk? Back then we called

the insect infestation *ferros*, thinking of Hebrew
captivity in Egypt and believing they were chanting
free us, instead of the *come hither* recent science

insists on, but who can dismiss the thought
that some fifty years back their ancestors dinned
a river of sound all night, extending lament

to lamentation, and I am shaken by the thought
of how easy it is for me to sit here under sharp
stars which could mark in heaven the graves

of tortured boys and inhale the dregs of expensive
whiskey the color of a fox, how convenient
to admit where no light shows my safe face

that I have been less than innocent this entire
life and never gave a second thought to this:
even the window fan cooling my bedroom

stirs the air with *blades*, and how could anyone
in a civilized nation ever be condemned for
narrowing breath to melody between the teeth,

and if this is an exercise in sham shame I am
feeling, some wish for absolution, then I have to
understand the wave of nausea crossing me,

this conviction that it is not simple irony
making the whir of voices from the pine trees
now seem to say *Dar he, Dar he, Dar he.*

NOTE: Although most historians now concur that Mose
Wright said not "Dar he," but "There he is," the former is the
way his testimony was universally reported in the media, and it
has remained so in the public mind.

Carrion Cry

April summons a vulture flock
to our farm north of Goshen
for no particular reason,
unless it's the thawed fox
in the weeds by Whistle Creek
or some sin we can't name.
Like a throng of lost apostles
they perch in the peach trees
and preach a gospel so bleak
the ground is fouled slick.
The county agents apologize:
the bastards are sheltered
by federal law. Politicians,
buzzards—no difference to me.
There ought to be a bounty.
Hissing worse than bobcats,
they vomit and shit the yard
rancid. When the tabby flees
their roadkill reek, Delisa
won't open the drapes. "Bad
luck," she says and cuddles
her kitten. Their heads are
featherless to delve into death
and come up refreshed, sleek.
Sometimes in midday heat one
heretic opens his vast wingspan,
then smokes up to circuit ride

till his brotherhood follows,
their spirals shaping no wild
flower drifting down from Zion
but petals of a rogue-black rose
unfolding like a twisted word
spoiling over the orchard.

Wilson's Ivory-Bill

Coastal North Carolina, 1808

The third specimen the Scotsman shot
that day was barely damaged but crying
like a child, and he carried it under cover
into Wilmington, where women stared
from windows at the shocking sound.

He signed the register, *Alexander Wilson*
and child, but showed the landlord
his basketed find, then left the bird
in the room and went to tend his gelding,
which had been much frightened
by the captive's cries. Returning,
the astonished naturalist found a haze
of dust, and the red-crested hostage
(*full two feet long*, he later wrote)
hacking with the chisel tip of his beak
a hole in the plaster, exposing lath
and rattling the weatherboards,
whether from hunger or just hope
the collector did not know. He hobbled
his guest with twine and embarked
in search of some suitable fruit
for the *poule de bois*, not realizing
such a wild thing thrives on grubs,
persimmons, the seed of poison ivy.
Back empty-handed, he opened
the door to discover a tethered fury

wrecking the mahogany secretary.
It screamed—*yent, yent*—and locked
its captor with an irate yellow gaze.

Time to draw the curiosity in life,
he thought, while it still showed credible
vigor, and Wilson took many wounds
as he tried to adjust the woodpecker's
bellicose pose or open his wings wide.
He later reported the bird *displayed*
such a noble and unconquerable spirit,
that I was frequently tempted
to send him back to his native swamp.
For three days the artist persisted
in sketching and taking copious notes,
while the bird refused sustenance
and fell to silence and torpor.

He yearned to see the splendid creature
as a key to the eternal, a hint of Divinity's
all-embracing design but could not
forestall the inevitable and wrote,
years later, sapped himself by dysentery
and the hobgoblins of urban civility,
I grew ashamed of my belated pity
and witnessed the poor creature's death
with a measure of reverent regret.
On the verge of my own mortal demise
I am still haunted by his jonquil eyes.

The Restless Dead: Walker County, Georgia

I'd hoped to wake in glory, a bird returning
to the brightest limb in its dazzled mind.
I said, *Bless me and let my body disturb*
no earth, let my smoke braid as it ascends,
my ash just sleep. So often I had shoved
sourdough into the oven to make bread,
I had no fear of worldly flame. I wrote
my name on the dotted line and gave
the smiling undertaker his pay. I knew
he'd see to my needs in person—casket,
quiet combustion, a tasteful urn. Out here,
the owl scares me with its silent wings,
for I had wanted angels, not this swamp
of moss and stench, decaying remains
half floating in the fishing lake. How slow
this change I thought would be instant.
The light we all hope for is a fiction. Dark
is the rule when breath is ended, and life
still beckons—my sons, their sons crying
in the night, their wives weeping as again
they fill the kitchen to work a second wake.
Somewhere in the spirit realm my husband,
dear Harmon, waits. I want to cross over.
The state agents scurry with their shovels,
but rain keeps retrieval slow. How I yearn
to know I've slipped from this limbo
and into God's arms. The ghostly green

of a cherry willow weeping lends new
vigor to unsated wraiths. All gruesome sinew
and tallow, I am ashamed and want to hide
from hungry buzzards. I keep rehearsing
all my trespasses, my simmering sins,
and still cannot reckon this. Tonight I'll
ache, as we somehow can by moonlight,
toward the sound of the living as they're
dreaming. The redbuds wake now. Pale
dogwoods like bridal wreaths shine. One
bluebird gathers the sky's hue in a wing,
and I am left to fester and pine, left wanting
with every fiber to climb toward heaven,
to turn pure as sap and seep into the stem
of the scarlet trillium, into the bloom.
Is this what they mean by haunting?

Sump

Under the gristmill's wheel
the race spilled white as thistle,
and my face was held by a spell
in the pit's velvet water.
I was twelve, alone and chilled.

Every axle and ambered ratchet
of that grinding engine
held still as the eave's orb
of sleeping hornets, the miller
my father called brother was

two days dead, the weather
taut but dormant. Every woodland
bird was silent. The redbuds
bristled with petals, as I eased
my tongue over one syllable—

sump, all sibilant drone
and plosive. The oiled pawls
and gears whispered back,
sump, the slow dash of oak
into the sluice. Under pinions

with spindles, the bedstone
and running stone beckoned.
I could feel the damp planets

pivot in their blissful circles,
until a rat from curling ferns

edging the still water's rim
plashed into that black moat
to shatter my dim reflection—
strange face, glossy ripples,
a week without fresh meal.

As the first star rose and bristled,
the millrace shone and shirred.
I was learning the orbit of loss
on the eve of my first funeral,
the way kept water spoils.

Shepherd Ollie Strawbridge on the Chicken Business

Brothers, I have seen two Pruvells whirl a brown cyclone
in midair and slash their gaffs into each other for no cause
except God invented them for combat and no quarter,

and I have seen one blue-stripe flat-out assail a stupid man
who stepped between that bird and its close-bred cousin,
and they will flail at the mesh of cages for blood contact,

because that is the thought spinning in their pea-wit chicken
brains twenty-four-seven. And why the sheriff and his left-
wing backers believe a man like Cortez Darlington,

a deacon of long-standing in this fellowship and a businessman
of good faith, belongs behind bars for facilitating, I mean
just helping the gamecocks fulfill their natural destiny,

is more mystery to me than blood coming from church wine
or electric guitars whining the Gospel, because Cortez
loves those chickens and will leave a prayer meeting to save

them if a storm blows up, so why trust the tree-hugging
animal rights people who wouldn't know instinct if it
nipped them on the keister because their business is

getting into other humans' business until the sporting man
and sporting women and children, too, have to hide
their pleasure and keep secrets from their neighbors,

as if a fox and a coon and a red-tailed hawk was not
enough trouble to make fighting chickens a periled
way of putting bread on the table, and they are beautiful,

those red-headed birds with the question mark tails
and the gold feet, and for this reason before we sing
our next hymn which is "Christ My Soldier," I aim

to make a collection for Cortez who needs bail
something awful, and if we don't support our neighbor,
every each of us in Tazewell County and maybe

in this great commonwealth is in deep danger
of being surprised by the law at our work and cuffed
and told we're in violation. So let our spirits join

our brother in just violation and send him our prayers
and money, because George Washington himself
fought cocks and Andy Jackson brought his flock

to the White House carpet for scrimmage, and listen,
the fighting pit is not a site of sin, and the Bible
is on our side because it says God made the fowl

of the earth and gave man dominion, and a soul,
anyway, is not to be found in any ilk of chicken,
and we don't want to have to move hearth and home

and appetites to some Canada to be free. I know
Cortez also is charged with shotgunning a hawk
which is by law protected and with a forcible rape

they could never verify, but that is just the haves
planning against him, and the Lord's good scripture
is all we need to prove we are the loved ones

and the ones endangered, the species somebody
in Richmond wants wiped out, the free people,
the chosen and blessed, so now let's stand and reach

deep into our pockets, yes, and open the hymnals
and lift our voices for the Word and our brave new
world, praise Jesus, say amen. Now, page one-oh-one,

for a full-immersion anthem of our perilous survival.

Scuppernongs

Dusk in Monticello's autumn arbor—
the squire reaches into wasp-haunted
leaves to touch a single native grape
more treasured than *Muscat blanc*, catawba,
or *lacrimi dolci*. Seizing the evening,

he strolls the slate maze and terrace alone
to remember his late wife and lament
the decade he's struggled in vain to mate
the Old World delicates to *Vitus
vulpina*, the fragrant grape Aesop's fox

would have said anything just to taste.
"The homely scuppernong," he thinks, "is
dusky, Southern, its ruminant juices rife
with a sweetness indigenous to any
Edenic muscadine tribe, yet immune

to local perils like the aphid, black rot,
powdery mildew, fretters." He moves
through spider floss and spike dandelions.
"Unrefined," he judges, "but with vigor,"
and yearns to wed the spirits of a neighbor's

low-brow tendrils to the courtesies
of Europe—nuance, dry insinuation,
a widower's oblique ardor. Ruminant

himself, graying russet, Jefferson maintains
a sovereign's posture and is stepping

in dew now through the garden pavilion
to spy the Marseilles fig espaliered,
limbs twisted, crucified. A spilling fountain
silvers. Late birds trill. Sunset is polished
with jeweler's rouge, a French touch. The wind

stiffens his shoulders as the planter turns
back to the wicker gate, threshold, the hearth,
and flame, the thought of a mulled aperitif,
the violin waiting by the lampstand,
and then his threadbare mourning shawl

already warmed by Sally's serving hands.

A Pentecostal Note

First it was only a rhythm of wind
in the sour oaks and hagwood,
last year's leaves still chattering
about the dying winter, so I kept
lifting the leftover splits of hickory,

moving the stack, good steward
that I am, to mow the first rampant
grasses of March. When a flat
tablet of poplar shingling a cozy
gap slid aside, a halo of slow braid

stirred, a small timber snake, head
rearing like a Clovis stone and rattles
shuddering their revival tambourine.
I did a deft step then, jumped back
like a soul touched to the quick

by the spirit and the light. I spoke
in tongues with no design. It was
a holy moment, I'm here to witness,
so I quit work early to savor
that shivery hymn and deliverance.

It seemed a good time, if one exists,
to reflect on minor revelations
and the sudden agencies of praise,

though I confess, as the horizon
reddened I backslid something serious,

pouring Jack Daniels into a glass,
doubling my whisky ration,
thinking in the wake of a mild shock,
No such thing as a tall drink,
a short snake, or a temperate vision.

Outsider Art

The felon who saved wooden matchsticks
bartered from cellmates to craft this chapel
worked slowly in sparse light with a locksmith's
fingers. What he used as glue is already

a mystery, probably some gray paste
whipped up in the kitchen from cornstarch
and chicken grease. The church is a marvel—
solid, polished, flush, and plumb, its symmetries

and surprises, I imagine, sketched
for practice on a steel wall. Touching it,
I can't help wonder how many smuggled
coffin nails were lit to render the miniscule

timber, pine sticks with the scorch-end snipped.
What was he in for, anyway? I picture
two hearts tattooed blue as a lucifer's tip,
a gray beard grizzled rough as emery,

his fingers nimble enough to read Braille.
The steeple is perfect, the portal cross,
pitched roof, chancel windows backed with foil.
By day did he scrub laundry or pound rocks?

He knew what it meant to be confined by work
and freed by form. He watched every inmate

lighting up, match tips flared by friction,
the sulphur and phosphorous of brimstone,

and yet he raised a holy house to convey
his patience. Meticulous, he could not shake
or waver, shaping what had been blown
out to conjure visions of escaping smoke.

House of sleeping fire tempting any spark,
his unkindled pyre, it lit the prison dark.

The Booth Prism

Dramatis Personae:

Abraham Lincoln—assassinated wartime president to whom freedom was not a slogan but an idea/ Andrew Johnson—Lincoln's successor with less generous intentions/ John Wilkes (Johnny, Pet, Wilkes, etc.) Booth—an actor and zealot both onstage and off/ Junius Brutus Booth—father of the assassin and most famous American Shakespearean actor of his day/ Edwin Booth—an older brother of J.W.B. and his father's successor as acclaimed Shakespearean/ Junius [June] Booth Jr.—another sibling thespian and theatrical manager / Joseph Booth—another brother of J.W.B., eventually a doctor/ Asia Booth Clarke—beloved sister of J.W.B./ John Sleeper [Jack] Clarke—comedic actor and husband to Asia/ Clara Morris—popular actress who often worked with Booth/ Lucy Hale—Booth's putative fiancée/ Isabel Sumner—a Boston grocer's daughter, sixteen in 1864, when she and J.W.B. corresponded and enjoyed a rendezvous in New York/ Mary Surratt—Confederate-sympathizing widow hanged as part of the Lincoln assassination conspiracy/ Anna Surratt Tonry—her daughter/ John [Johnny] Surratt—Confederate spy and plotter, son of Mary, eventually captured and exonerated on the same evidence that condemned his mother/ Clara—Surratt servant/ Boston Corbett—hatter, zealot, soldier, prisoner of war, the killer of Booth

Booth: A Quick History

"As animals in a pack hasten after their sovereign,"
wrote one costar, "so we followed him." He was,
after all, "a Beau Brummell, but robust" in the eyes

of one reviewer. The ninth child, the favorite, he chose
his father's profession and with his swashbuckling style
became America's matinee idol. A quick wit and adroit

horseman, he insisted on stage swordplay so violent
he was often wounded and bore many scars, though not all
critics were impressed with his elocution. Nonetheless,

when he stepped out limping as Richard or blackfaced
for the Moor, his anthracite eyes in the limelight flashed
like Mesmer's, and ladies in the front row swooned.

He held his liquor well and guaranteed good box office
from St. Louis to Boston, but while he flourished
during the war, his views on slavery grew more fiery,

and he was not one to hold his tongue about how
"King Lincoln" was a tyrant. History casts him as misfit,
but he rode a crest of success until Gettysburg,

a prosperous celebrity, though his love of the Confederacy
led him to anger and brandy. After Lee's surrender
he saw everything as theater and tragedy. He never

understood why even the Southern press turned on him
after his brash act. Even that last morning he deemed
himself a wounded angel in the blazing barn. Brutus

was his model, and on his deathbed he begged his mother
be spared the details. He was twenty-six. After a hasty
autopsy, he was buried under a dungeon, but for decades

acquaintances claimed to meet him in Hong Kong, Paris,
or the brothels of New Orleans, while an effigy alleged
to be his mummy toured the country in sideshows

billed as *Remains of the Villainous Assassin*. Bad luck—
ruin or fire—followed every owner of that grisly display,
but the crowds came, rain or shine. They stood in line

for hours and whispered, appalled, as they waited to pay.

Ebony: John Wilkes Booth Recites "The Raven"

In cold Louisville to commit eloquent murder
and be praised, he rehearsed before the mirror—
Richard's winter of discontent, Macbeth, the Moor.
His train the week before delayed by blizzard,
he'd fought off black wolves, as he later claimed,
and paid a sleigh driver to haul him over snow.
At Corby's back in St. Joe he had closed the card
with an encore from Tennyson's cavalry charge,
but he must have craved something darker after
his own bleak December. It was a slow Tuesday,
January nineteenth, and if he knew the birthdays
of Robert Lee and Poe converged, he never said,
yet he did change his program. Bronchial problems
persisting since Christmas had altered his delivery
and pitch, and the winter tour had left him weary.
Perhaps his lowered register, the new romance
of a damaged instrument, lured him to the poem.

His father, Junius Brutus, had heard once in person
the poseur he called "The Nevermore" and seen
the urban ladies swoon over "that contraption,
of sham melancholy and gothic gesture," and yet,
he asked his bastard sons—all apprentice actors—
to add the verses to their memory store. Wilkes
would have seen the ebony bird as both omen
and threat, for even at Tudor Hall, the sullen boy
had come to scorn black servants and ordered
them to bow. He called them *curs* and stormed

about for hours when a maid or valet cowered,
his disposition drawing him to resent even hints
of abolition. Brooding on future fame, he adored
lost maidens and plantations twilit with wisteria,
Jacobean dialogue, and other bits of curious lore
but was never in love with death, as admirers
reeling in stunned disbelief would afterward attest.

Booth was called the American Adonis and played
to packed houses, his brooding glamour magnified
in the lens of opera glasses. Scholars had praised
his Romeo, though one critic quipped, "His oratory
seldom equals his rapier play." A known *bon vivant*,
he excelled at target practice and banter, served brandy
fit for a prince, and wrote his mother near the close
of a triumphant tour, "My goose does indeed hang high."
He jested with the pet names of stage-door *grisettes*
and debutantes alike. That week at Woods Theater
there was little to protect him from their desperate
notes and flowers. The evening before, he'd polished
off a flask of cognac in the green room and succumbed
to the charms of a jade who arrived with an armload
of roses. He japed the following morning, "I wore
the camel hump of Crookback Dick, but wished
for Othello's silk regalia to mimic the pillow scene."

When the moment arrives, the velvet curtain rustling
behind him and purple, applause succumbs to silence,
a cough, then a deeper hush. He stands downstage
in immaculate black, traces of the Moor's burnt cork

smudging his neck over a silk cravat. The auditorium
is still tainted with echoes of the black ram tupping
a white ewe. "Edgar Poe's poem 'The Raven,'" he says,
"yet another tale of a lady lost." He raises the shut
book in his hand. It is, in fact, Marlowe's *Tamburlaine*.
He pauses, preening, touching his new moustache.
"Once upon a midnight dreary, while I pondered weak
and weary . . . ," he recites, eyes fixed on something
in midair before him. The spell is set as Booth's
brooding voice moves through the lines, but his mind
wanders to his adopted motherland's demise,
the *Richmond Examiner*'s report from New Year's
Eve: *Today closes the gloomiest year of our struggle.*

The Gettysburg disaster, Chattanooga fallen, the Ape
offering amnesty to any rebel raising the white feather—
and with that thought, his voice a lute in tremolo,
he begins to flaw the lines, to stray and splice
the lyric with the play. The "rare and radiant maiden"
is Desdemona accused, the "very error of the moon"
what lures an ominous bird of yore. Not one noise
from the wings or pit attempts to prompt him back,
as he is given to such flights from script. The jet
of his moustache and pomaded hair shine, as smoke
from the wan gaslights wafts. Soon he has laced
the woeful ballad's grieving scholar with actions
whose passage "will make bond-slaves and pagans
our statesmen." Eyes closed and broad brow knit,
he gapes and wavers as if in trance over some grief
half recalled or the deadly hex cast from a Gulf

Coast conjure, as if in dreams no mortal dared ever
dream before. Each scrap of the dark poem weds

the Bard, as Poe's narrator wishing to raise the dead
alludes to savage men whose heads grow beneath
their shoulders. A lady gasps. Lisping whispers rise
and crest like waves. The actor pauses to produce
a silk kerchief as black as any raven, and every
eye in the room watches it sway in grim cadence
with the poem. Can anyone understand or read
the rude future in flourishes of his distress,
the echoes of homicide as Othello's rage revives?
He paces, losing lines, wasting them on curtains,
the polished floor, the chandeliers. Suddenly, Booth
freezes, shifts his weight to scan the rows for allies,
rivals, the sheen of a malignant bird or beaked face
of an owlish Athena. And then, as everyone
present will remember next year and forever after,
he staggers and proclaims, "'Tis a pageant to keep us
in false gaze. If we loose the chains, dark dangers
abound. Oh yes, I'll smile and smile and be . . . ,"

but a frantic stage hand appears to rush him
away behind a gaze that conveys, "Sorry, one dram
of brandy too many." The worried murmurs circulate
and house lights rise. "The black poem," they wonder,
"the doomed poet: is his curse passed to our favorite?"
What gossip will follow can only increase interest
in his next performance, and some who sat in boxes
close by the stage swore the last syllables they heard

from behind the drapes were Booth's and ghoulish
and shrieking, "on horror's head horrors accumulate."
And some will say—a few—they heard amid the echo
of that despairing word—*Nevermore*—a thrashing
of great wings in the shadows, followed by the din
heard only when some dire bird of prey has seized
his victim and wheels away, dark feathers rushing
to the kingdom from which no traveler ever returns.

Next day, however, sober over demitasse and pastry,
he said, "Our only hope now lies in saving slavery,"
and ran off to rehearse the role of Charles de Moor
in *The Robbers*, a role he chose to perform as comedy,
despite the director's brisk admonition: "Remember,
sir, you must not play so light, for this is murder."

Exhuming Booth

When Booth the future assassin strutted and sulked his adequate Hamlet,
the ladies in the front row swooned. "The handsomest man in America,"
the *Boston Herald* called him, and he insisted on swordplay so violent
his body was mapped with scars. He loved his pocket flask, his diamond
stickpin and yellow foxskin cap. Had his target, "Ape" Lincoln, turned
in his rocker, he would have greeted the man, "Good evening, Mr. Booth."

That railsplitter loved drama and comedy alike and admired the whole
Booth family of madcap actors. He had met Wilkes once and shook
his hand. Popular history calls the player mediocre, disappointed, mad,
but Wilkes had star status, an ivory-tipped cane, hair lustrous as a raven.
The actress Clara Morris wrote, "At the theater, as sunflowers turn
upon their stalks to follow the beloved sun, so old and young our faces

smilingly turned on him." He loved the South and women, especially
the tarts at Ella Starr's sporting house near the capitol, and men praised
his manners, his equitation, fencing, and diction. He was a lively
companion and known to be sharp with a gun. Yet he was restless,
and ambition would not let him sleep. He took physic and paced,
saying over and again the lines of Richmond, Shylock, and Claudius.

And yes, he lived in his father's shadow and could not get warm.
He prospered during the war but grew strange, furtive, spent thousands
on quinine for Confederate wounded. "His palms were rough," his friend
Mears wrote, "from oaring a boat through mist to deliver the forbidden."
He could have been wild as Byron but insisted his valet clip names
off any letter from a "true lady." He would not compromise an admirer,

and yet he had stage-door lovers, dozens of assignations and trysts.
But what was he thinking those last months, downing French brandy
by the tumbler to whisper over candlelight his avenging schemes?
His comrades were fools and felons. Born a bastard, he once showed
his palm to a gypsy, who said, "You have a dangerous hand." As a spy,
he was a failure, but years after a sergeant shot him in a blazing barn,

he was reported lurking in taverns from the Gulf to Singapore.
In his diary he had written, "I do not wish to shed a drop of blood,
but I must fight the course. 'Tis all that's left me," the last words
Macbeth's. Fevered, his shank badly broken, he stood in the barn,
taunting the wrathful cavalry. They struck match flare to fodder corn,
and he leaned on crutches under an arc of fire beyond the theatrical.

His moustache was gone. Mr. Boyd said he was surely a demon
framed in flame. One soldier claimed to hear the voice of God
commanding, so he shot. The bullet entered the neck, spinning
downward to pierce three vertebrae and sever Booth's spinal cord.
Under the apple tree they placed him on a straw mattress. "Kill me,
oh, kill me," he said, then, "Tell mother I died for my country. I did

what I thought was best." As dawn embered over the Rappahannock,
the blazing Garrett barn collapsed. Everyone remembers the words
he cried that Good Friday night: *Sic Semper Tyrannis.* From Brutus,
and Virginia's state seal. During the autopsy by Doctor Barnes,
his head came detached. The body was thrown into a musket case,
nailed shut and shoveled under the Old Penitentiary's cellar floor.

Carnivals claimed to display the skull: *The Mind of the Monster!*
Spectators wanted to see the brain's convolutions, others to touch
the cranium and measure it, to anatomize in a sterile academy

and apply the tenets of anthropometry or intuit the man's nature,
his *phrenos*, from the white dome's lunar map. Would it matter?
Maxilla and fossae, parietal slope, the malar bone that harbors

the eye? How much is simply chemical? He believed in slavery
as a way to enforce order. He did murder and cheated the gibbet.
Men of judgment looked him in the eye and saw not a glimpse
of the riddle. Smitten women wore his hair over their hearts,
but why would Providence allow such a twist of spirit,
a nightmare walking among celebrating citizens? In the torch-lit

streets after Appomattox what reveler could guess his intent?
Was there some music swarming inside him, a miserable shift
like the light of a migraine? Some say *evil genius*, but Silsbee's
ambrotype hints only of Narcissus, perhaps a cad, elegance at ease,
though the eyes never quite match. That evening before Easter
when he leapt to the stage, one wheel spur caught a draped banner,

the rowel ripping an oil portrait of Washington. His eyes blazed
in the footlights, as if Richard, his essential, brilliant character,
had at last sloughed costume and script, all props but the dagger,
to certify destiny's dependence on lightning, a brimstone glare
from a photographer's flashpan. Were shame and forgiveness
missing from his moral education? Perhaps his personal effects

witness how close his thirst for beauty brought him to the abyss:
revolvers, a knife and pipe, Yankee dollars, and pictures of women.
And finally, with its pilot's rose and needle, his rusting compass.
His last words were the whisper of wind across a velvet curtain—
useless, useless—a shadow over ice, an owl's wing, the hiss
of a quenched limelight, the spectral spiral of fugitive smoke.

Keepsake

Of the many who wore clippings of his hair
in lockets because he had been their matinee
Hamlet, some chose to dispose of the strands,

though others saw how any oddment of evil
might fetch a handsome price, and he was seen,
overnight, to have been a villain all along.

Nonetheless, the escape was romantic—broken
leg bone, a scrap of Latin, a waiting horse.
For years his manservant had sold stray tendrils—

even clippings from the mane of his mare—
to society women who fanned their bosoms
and schemed to meet him, to glean a souvenir.

Some, in distress, may have buried their tokens
or burned the hair in private. One lock, however,
was the saddest artifact, for Senator Hale's

daughter, courted by John Hay and Todd Lincoln,
had in the public parlor of the National Hotel
fallen for the actor and consented, under the spell

of his dark charm, to marry in the coming season.
Her doting father, a new-tapped ambassador,
disapproved and vowed to spirit her to Spain.

Shocked by the breaking news of Wilkes' role
in the murder, she pled in print for evidence
of his innocence, then swore to wed him,

if necessary, in the scaffold's shadow.
The night when the actor's body was smuggled
from that rural conflagration and his final

gasping soliloquy, Miss Hale, under escort
and heavily veiled, was led aboard the Monitor
Montauk and allowed to view the gruesome

corpse. An officer, it is said, pulled aside
the torn horse blanket, and when Booth lay thus
unshrouded in the watchman's lantern beam,

the lady whose name no one uttered began
to wail like a widow and shiver. Only then
did the young lieutenant sever a ringlet

for her with his penknife. Years later, Lucy,
truly widowed and back at last from Spain,
whispered to a familiar that any book

or stage drama daring to offer her story
since that stony moment should bear the title
A Dead Woman's Life. She wore only

black after that, grew addicted to charities,
kept her treasure who-knows-where? and refused,
as was the custom of the time, all interviews.

And who can fathom the mysteries of shrift?
The rumors say she suffered from spent nerves
and always wore beneath her simple shift
a pendant—inscribed in floral cursive *I forgive.*

Booth from Beyond

Seventeen, star-struck and affluent, having swooned
at his Hamlet, Miss Isabel Sumner visited the actor
in his chamber and wrote letters he answered
with a swain's eloquence and nothing of the assassin:
"I know the *world*, my dear, and had begun to hate it.
I saw you, Things seemed changed." He asked her
with his best conventional diction not to play
upon his heart with "a Girl's caprice, the mere
pastime of an hour" and swore, "Your sweet face
could move me to do anything." She sent flowers
and her blessing, but he vanished into the tragedy
he composed on venom and brandy. The papers
painted him a monster, *sic semper tyrannis* the zeal
of a fevered mind. But later, sipping on memories
of that evening in his arms, the souvenirs dueling
on stage had written on his body, she knew the eyes
were in torment and carried a paper with his name
inscribed in code to Madame LaDoux in Boston,
who was said to conjure the voices of the dead.
Summoned, he whispered secrets, how "Uncle Ape"
was plotting to burn the South and send his Negroes
raping. The frail spirit wept to see her engaged
to a trader named Dunbar. "Beware the Beacon Street
gentry," he echoed. "The foxes will tear your soul
with simpering dignity. Remember, he loves
his country more than gold or life. Thus Brutus,
thus Booth." He said the Styx is not so soothing

as the Rappahannock, and "Do you yet wear the ring
of pearl inscribed with our linked initials?" And if
he ever came again, she kept her own council. Smiling
at clouds from a lounge years later, while facing death
in the Fairfax Hotel, she offered her one daughter this,

"He was pure genius and beautiful, though almost evil.
Whatever mortal agent aimed him to such infamy
never knew of the healing angel he burned to be.
His *carte de visite* is best consigned to flame,
for this is another era. The secret dies with me."
A beckoning candle seemed to offer counterclaim.

Site Visit: Ford's Historic Playhouse

When you visit Ford's Theater, as I trust
you will, the neoclassical pilasters facing
Tenth Street will leave you unimpressed.
The bricks are chipped and distressed,
etched with the cruel edge of our history.
Passing, then, through a door to the salon
and lobby whose opulence will astonish,
you will notice a plaque's brass apology:
The luxurious décor of Ford's famous theater
is far superior to the unfinished exterior.
Perhaps you will respond, if only in silence,
that Lincoln himself was so construed.

As you approach the narrow vestibule
and then the presidential box, the question
Why? will already assail you, since the war
was over, leaving the actor's beloved South
protected only by the Liberator's aptitude
for mercy. Be that as it may, Booth had lately
been crazed with hatred for one he believed
favored imperial rule. The brash assassin,
as books and color brochures testify,
was affluent, dashing, a famous face called
by one reporter "America's new Romeo."
Madness, it seems, ran rampant in his family.

He was at home in this theater and once,
rumor has it, refused after a performance
of *The Marble Heart* to meet and shake

the hand of his "tormentor." "I had rather,"
he said, "have the applause of a nigger,"
as if such venom were a sign of wit.
Familiar with the slack habits of the sentry,
he slipped along the passage, a shadow
smiling in stealth, fortified by raw brandy
—cliché, yes, but essential to the story—
a Derringer of large caliber and one scrap
of Latin borrowed from a flag. Desperation
cold as his has spelled the end of many.
No doubt a dark melody suffused his brain.

The original rocker with which the President
kept cadence like a cradle's from overture
to the "last act" is missing and under custody
of the Ford estate in Dearborn, but the replica
is enough to stop your heart—the feminine
pattern and back padding. The tufted sofa
and Turkish carpet, sash and valance, all
the yellow curtains and Nottingham lace
convey the luxury, the sense of safety,
as "Father Abraham" had scoffed at threats.
The banners and chandeliers will reinforce
the sense of vintage civility. All in black,
Booth seemed a carrion bird. *Our American
Cousin*, that night's play, is a comedy.

Booth twisted its history into a tragedy
of revenge with his shot and shout, the leap
most any matinee gallant playing the paladin
would envy. Did he break his shin bone?

He managed to reach his horse in the alley.
The aftermath was, of course, a frenzy,
the dying statesman at that time despised
by many hauled across the street, blood
seeping from the skull. The First Lady
wept so hard she had to be carried. Ford
himself was arrested as the night's other
assigned deeds unfurled, and the assassin
fled through marshes and slept in sheds.

Surveying the orchestra pit, the long rows
of seats, an exquisite auditorium famous
for its ventilation, you cannot but imagine
the stench of limelight, brutal acoustics
of a firearm's echo, the audience drawing
a collective breath, as sconced gaslights
flickered like hell itself. This was shock
drama so unembellished Shakespeare
would not have staged it. Cold, fevered
in Zekiah swamp, Wilkes, as his friends
called him (though his family preferred
Johnny), was desperate to see newspapers.

A star, he was eager to read the reviews
and expected congratulations and envy.
But before you leave, you will perhaps
remember how he was cornered at dawn
in a tobacco barn, leaning on his crutch,
defying commands to surrender. The shot,
against orders, severed his spinal cord,
and the assassin's assassin reported, "God

Almighty whispered that I must kill him."
No tour of the Theater is complete without
this reminder: a detective with the cavalry
who tracked him down, wrote much later,

"We set the barn afire, and when he stood
in the doorway waving his fist, he looked
for all the world like great Helios there, aglow,
showing nor fear nor shame. He was trimmed—
I shall never forget it—in unearthly flame."
One doubts the prudence of such enthusiasm,
and the bitter chapters followed, conspirators
and suspects quickly hanged, Reconstruction
and revenge, the nation's phoenix years,
decades Twain would brand a Gilded Age.
The theater, too haunted to entertain,
soon filled with rats and mildew, dust
and indigents. The jailed owner had been
released, though the curse of that Good
Friday never allowed him easy sleep.
The song echoing in his mind held more
horror and sorrow than a dozen cellos
can muster, and though the arena prospers
today in other hands and every glance
reveals a wealth of plush appointments
far more elegant than before, you will not
be tempted to say this visit was a pleasure
or praise it with the nickname—fatal irony—
Booth's public preferred. When he bowed
they shouted to him and threw flowers
at his feet. *Beauty*, they called him, *Beauty*.

God touched my shoulder. I was chosen.
That morning in Virginia was not my first time.
In the Gehenna they called Andersonville
He whispered, and I commenced to preach against
the she-dragon's presence. The sun, hunger, filth,
but the worst was more vile, a wickedness invented
by the sons of men. They betrayed one another
and showed tunnels to the Judas spies. Ransom
and bounty were salt and quinine. No loyalty
could stop them, and the stockade began to seethe
murder and flies. When I raised my tongue to Zion,
despite maggots in the meager cush and drinkage
downstream from the guards' latrine, I sowed
the Word, my fruit better than fine gold, revenue
sweeter than choice silver. My gospel helped
ease the passage of the perishing, and Rebel
sentries bet on my fellow prisoners bashing me,
but the Lord looks after His precious own.
He smiled and gave me the sharpshooter's eye.

The blasphemer in the barn taunted us all. Dawn
was red streak-o-lean in the holy east. A squad
from the Sixteenth New York under Doherty,
we were seasoned cavalry and eager. All night
in the saddle, I kept saying, *Tell me, Lord, give me
a sign.* They did not call me the Glory-to-God
Man for nothing, and Booth's bullet had shaken
Heaven's pillars. He postured in his black suit,

crutch like a weapon, and the words he snarled
were from Hell, defiant and thorned with laughter.
I knew him for the Devil's vessel, an actor
who consorted with whores. When my Rachel
died, I made purity my ambition but once backslid
with a brace of harborside doxies. Next morning
I used scissors to prevent repeating that ruin.
The doctors called it the Hatter's Madness
from mercury fumes that turned me radical, but God
has His own manners. Then the war saved me,
gave me a new task. I stood uniformed upon a caisson
to castigate Hooker's camp followers. Soldiers
are easy marks for the swift fiddler and scents
of the slag Sheba. I gave them Isaiah and a charm
against harlots. Heathens and Jezebels granted me
a wide path, but I fought Mosby and other phantoms
till Andersonville's scarecrows were avenged.

Lincoln's butcher was already a ghost before I raised
my pistol. The Apocalypse of a ramshackle burning
barn could not contain him. God's gelding, I knew
my destiny was wed to his. Smoke and shadows.
That voice. Hammer back like a bantam's crest,
sights lined up and the cold barrel level—I touched
the trigger gently. Under the stunted apple tree
where they carried him, he spoke little, his spine
severed by the divine projectile, but any man jack
could see Satan in his eyes. His wallet was a gallery
of tintype women, and they are all deceivers, soft
instruments of decay. *Useless*, he whispered, *useless*,

the serpent's hiss, the lure of insidious hopelessness.
The burley flames were leaping behind us, the sky
washed to brandy, his breath desperate. Into his ear
I poured scripture while one Lucinda Holloway,
reputed a local beauty, bathed his brow. The spirit
leaking away gave his face a glow, the shining out
of sheer evil. I would do it again. She gave him
a rose and muttered, *Such a pity*. They shackled me
and charged I was an accomplice rescuing renegade
Jeff Davis from links to the villain. No officer issued
the order I heard, nor could they conceive the chain
of command I obeyed. I was locked in Hell again.
It was familiar as daily prayers, but when conspiracy
talk gave way to grief, I was accorded reward and freed,
though the humble shop and hatter's trade of Samuel
Mason could no longer hold me, and I wandered
like unto a wild ass turned to the thicket. His voice
was the lodestone, and I roamed the barrens, always
dreaming like Pharaoh of the lean kine, comrades
who wasted away as convicts, so many brought low
by women who urged them to seek glory in holy war.

In the sharp mountains or plains of bowing grasses
aflame, I see the Father's hand soothing and smiting,
feel his wise wrath star-crested and embered.
Always God has told me to rejoice, for I have
broken the bow of Edom, I have slain the harlot's
darling, and if men embrace plague and pestilence,
I do not share the blame. Here under the peaks
I worship and show pilgrims the image Brady's

apprentice made of me. I am the sworn angel,
and they line up to purchase my tonics and ask
for autographs. Drifting, I survive on manna
and minor fame, the fate of Heaven's messenger.
Now the harvest is passed and summer is ended.
While ice blossoms in grass like teeth of a beast,
the righteous and fiendish alike suffer hunger,
and we are not any of us saved unless we trust
scripture and His voice in the whirlwind or cloud
saying, *Exhort the faithful, scourge the strumpet,
pull the trigger, chosen one. Welcome the shroud.*

Asia

Dear Sophie,

"Job's Tears" was the quilt I gave Wilkes
the year we failed at farming, but he could not,
he said, bear the sorrow in the pattern. Father
gone, dear mother almost smothered in widow's
weeds, melancholy haunted him already. Those
were prosy days, as we struggled with our *Memoir
of Booth the Elder*, since published, of course,
under my name alone—Asia B. Clarke. Benign
enough, I trust. We read Hawthorne, Milton,
and Plutarch to distract us. We studied
butterflies and lightning bugs Wilkes swore were
carrying a sacred torch. A mild boy, and yet,
in the wake of our mad sire's demise,
he took the master's staff and ledger, Prince Hal
rising to the crown, though his heart was pledged
to the stage. Agriculture, alas, was never
his strong suit, nor was he fond of the hunt,
but we made do, husbanding resources
with money scarce and conflict on the horizon.
We missed the ease of earlier days but found
pleasure elsewhere. I prompted him on *Caesar*
so often old Joe had half the lines by heart,
as all Tudor Hall's darkies played Anthony
and Casca in the swing seat under the willow.
As you know, assassination is the Bard's

bread and meat. A natural romantic, Wilkes
loved the rhetoric, which made him feel Roman.
But that is not what your sweet letter asks.

Therefore, this, my friend, for the record:
I never guessed at the plot nor heard him utter
anything of murder. Of his sense of mission,
however, I was not wholly in the dark. So many
nights he slept on our sofa in those high boots
with sewn-in holsters and counseled strangers
in the parlor all ungodly hours. They called
him "Doctor," and when I inquired, he confessed
to carrying quinine in horse collars to his Rebels,
chamomile, morphia, all manner of contraband.
His hands were hard from rowing the Potomac—
night work, cavalier foolery, but it was
Grant's pass that let him cross borders and ghost
between beliefs. Both South and North, the crowds
adored John Wilkes, and who can believe now
his autograph scarcely exists, so perilous to own
it in the vengeful frenzy. Lids shut, I remember
him acting Lady Macbeth's sleepwalking scene
in my long-trained dress. He seemed so harmless
elocuting in the woods, the very songbirds
transfixed, or galloping about on Cola
di Rienzi. His equestrian grace stamped him
a legend. Precious, he was our prince, but boys
from town called him Billy Bowlegs: Never
was he free from scoundrels' jeers. Always
ardent, he bore the gypsy's curse: a crone

confessed his palm alarmed her. "You were born,"
she said, "under a crossed star for a life riven
by thundering herds of enemies, a bad end,
but many will survive to mourn your loss."

That was his burden. Mine is speculation
and regret. I have no mystic glass to peer
into the conspiracy, but he drew followers
like a bellwether, and even under the Quaker
Lambs at Cockersville where we read history
and pauper's French he dreamed up mischief:
a squirrel in the proctor's desk, the alarm
bell's clapper swung for no earthly reason.
When the papers showed his cohorts—poor
Mrs. Surratt included—hooded, pendant
from the gallows, I wept to think how many
his absurd intrigue ushered through death's door,
and it was I who first showed him Foxx's
Book of Martyrs, which he clung to like a charm,
so I cannot altogether disavow the blame.

Listen, dearest Sophie, who can know the heart
of a son of Brutus? Mother's vision was prophesy:
Our hearth flame up-lept like a wave of blood,
then blazed *country* and his name just two days
before his birth. Omens, ill luck. Still, one asks,
"Why him?" He loved the village dance and camp
meetings, nibbling sweet roots and twigs he called
his "burrowing," and the blunderbuss in his room,
our only gun, was no more than a jest to him,
and yet a chamber in his brain was ever

shut snug as a coffin. How quickly his star
ascended. One day we were gathering mandrakes
and May apples, the next he was swaggering
across the stage, shooting sparks from the hazel
of his eyes. Who ventured to discover the verdure
there? Lukewarm reviews gave way to praise,
and even cautious Edwin admitted such applause
was rare and presaged a monumental future.

I suppose you know how the provost marshal
went rabid swiftly upon that horrid Good Friday—
curfews, searches, no mercy, everyone arrested,
my guiltless husband in hard custody,
a detective assigned to my lying-in chamber
as the labor pains came fiercer and faster.
(One twin was to bear Wilkes' name, but after
the event we assayed to bury every connection.)
His assets and manifesto in our iron safe
offered ample evidence to some, so we fled,
with no irony, back to father's England, where
I hide my heritage behind a mourning veil,
while Haymarket crowds applaud Jack's clowns
and drunkards. He has them chortling in the aisles,
and the fool's art sells tickets by the thousand;
but it is hardly acting, and I endure his icy
indifference the best I can. Pride, brandy,
and mistresses, cavalcades of hansoms
to Piccadilly, diamonds and dining by the river—
fame brings its madness and will not be denied.
Since the day he was thrown into prison
for being wed to the sibling of an assassin,

Jack has been cold as a knife in my presence,
and I am left to make do, receiving neighbor
ladies ignorant of my pedigree, the blood
traced from my veins to . . . whose? Iago's?
They coo and croon and preen. They dally
endlessly over gossip and provincial folly,
counting me their equal. I keep my secret
and despise fat, greasy-voiced, fair-whiskered
Britons and their pigeony prattle. My heart
is not here. For sanity, I keep my holidays
American, though I concede the irony.
Edwin writes monthly, with clippings of his *Hamlet*
acclaim, but will not set down his brother's name.

And, "Why?" fanatics still ask. "Why Booth?"
"Why Lincoln?" I am convinced he unhinged after
reading of the president in Richmond, strutting
the conqueror. That city was the site of Wilkes'
first success, and the man would have become King
Abraham, Sophie, and yearned to see his enemy
capital in ashes. There were other, wiser paths.
He might, for instance, have mourned for the South,
might have taken the humble victor's route,
as Grant did, and refused to cross the Rubicon
with his legions. He might have prayed. Piety
so becomes a conqueror. But he had to parade
in the fallen city, to wave his bloody
banner along Shockoe Bottom and the cemetery
of fresh martyrs. Wilkes' heart had already
hardened to sorrow, but he still had fury,
and when he heard, they say all prudence fled.

I know his act was evil, his warm nature
turned quixotic, but those were years of madness,
war fever, and opprobrium of defeat.
Whose actions were judicious? Whose causes
could now be argued, in hindsight, with pride?
Where once the sad Africans were enslaved,
now their masters fared little better under
the heel of vengeful zealots in Congress.
And yet, I know freedom is justice, murder
of even an enemy against the will of God.
The viperous times made so many monsters.
Would that Wilkes had taken to heart more holy
scripture and less theatric Shakespeare.

So is it in the blood, the Tragic Booths of Hell?
Sophie, I confront such deadly questions daily,
and how quickly I learned to live with injury.
Rumors painting me mad ossified to legend
before we could devise our family strategy:
They said I raved in a private asylum, I was dead,
dying, shivering in morphine addiction.
The stories multiplied like forest hares.
Some said I harbored the plot, a Rebel harpy.
I expected to be stoned or shot, and more
than once the well-heeled citizens spat at me.
Old friends were shocked to see me walking free.
What choice but to sail for England? Yet misfortune
is an avid tracker and found its foul way here.
I should not be surprised. Our destiny
was mapped tragic. We children were all born
of illicit passion. Father had another wife,

you've no doubt heard. Like him, pure English.
"Now gods, stand up for bastards!" our Edmund
said. How Wilkes struggled with the infamy
of our birth. Even now, my tea trembles,
the cup and saucer rattling like a serpent.
"*Sic semper tyrannis*," he said, the Old Dominion's
motto. I miss him still, the boy who embraced
the sadness in a jew's harp as Joe twanged out
a tuneless noise in the dark kitchen. His palms
raw from clenching milk through Lady Parker's
dry dugs, my brother wished to see the world
enchanted. After father's last escapade, the liquor
winning out, as we feared it would, Wilkes scored
in fine India ink his own initials in his hand,
"to remember who we are and are not," he said,
but he imagined us part of the flowery South.
He came to hate black Irish who rushed in droves
to free bond slaves. Horrified at anything
not elegance or honor, he was the shooting star
whose demise undid us all. Bastille days—decoys,
detectives, and all that vile rabble of human
bloodhounds infesting the city. June arrested,
Joseph and my husband. A plague on all their
houses, the bounty seeking ravens and minions
of the vicious. Now I peer across new snow
at the sparrow-colored copse and yearn for a past
when we built our stage beneath the arbor,
despite father's wish we would not be actors,
and there we strutted and fretted in innocent
make-believe much saner than the masquerade

I now endure. If only I had seen how apt the quilt
I sewed from scraps of old costumes—Hamlet's
weeds, Othello's robe, the cloak Jack Falstaff
stumbled on. Back then Jehovah blessed us:
who would have imagined Job our emblem?

But one shot to the brain of a new-minted saint
ended all, the curtain fallen, gaslights quenched,
my own face haggard, smile erased, hair gray.
Think well of me, Sophie, exiled with my canary,
memory albums, and the meager comfort of dry
sherry in a cold and ever-showery country
where sorrow reigns. I harbor a tintype of Wilkes,
dashing in his cloak and moustache, but show it
to not a soul. Must love survive in secret?
A red bird preening on our frosted fence
beyond the window, as I look up from weary
words, spies his own aspect in the glass
and flees. Nothing lovely, it seems, can stay.
Please understand, my dear, not even innocence
resists time's havoc, and all bright yesterdays
fall prey to shadow. So runs the world away.
Would it be too wicked of us to wish for amnesia,
the chance to forget, forgive, and face a new dawn?
Be safe, and write a cheerful letter when you can.
So I remain

                    Your loving distant cousin,
                    Asia

Edwin Booth at the Players' Club: Portrait by John Singer Sargent, 1890

See the players well bestowed.
—HAMLET

I have no brother, I am no brother . . .
I am myself alone.
—RICHARD III

"Owling" again, as Edwin called it,
we talked of the late-night weather—
new snow soft on Gramercy Park—
as I sketched, conjuring the clock
back to show him at his zenith. The jets
hissed to dictate my light. Image fixed,
I primed, then worked nearly
in pure pigment with only the necessary
oil: his velvet jacket's aubergine,
high collar and cravat. The gaze
that transfixed half a century
and projected such mystery
from a sparrow of a man made radiant
by his voice. He posed before the dark
hearth. I gave the room an amber haze,
as if he were himself the fire's source.

It was his reckless brother, of course,
the name he would not utter,
as much as Denmark's royal curse,
murder in his history, dreams the color

of blood. "I am not by nature
nocturnal, but tragedy has made me famous,
and I cannot stroll the city unmolested."
And yet, he still basked in the glory
of his Hundred Nights of Hamlet,
as if Disaster were both kin and country.
He too had faced a crazed assassin
and wore the spent shot on his watchchain.

I have rendered him on the threshold
of a rhetoric that might explode—
a cocked pistol, black powder his element.
My intent? The Prince of Players, with Furies
hovering in the wings. Calcium flares
for isolation. Shadows hinting at Hals
and the pallor of a martyr from Valesquez.
Both genius and witness. His poise
was always on the verge of collapse.
Tact and damage augmented the strain.
"The readiness is all," he said. "Paint that."
Between the talons of truth and rumor,
he rehearsed Hamlet's paltry resolve,
a man, alas, on the brink of rancor.
He would play it to the grave.

Charm: Anna Surratt Tonry, 1900

When I envision my neighbor Nancy in chains
or lashed at the post for reading to her daughter,
I cannot imagine how we lent our allegiance
to even the notion of slaves, though Mother,
hearing of the emancipator's death, told soldiers
it must be punishment on a prideful people.
Always quick to chart the signs of God's justice,
she had to hang, or so it then seemed, all acts
that followed being but the natural consequence.
The source, however, of all our misfortune was Pet,
her name for the glamorous actor, and I admit
to being smitten myself. In my room I wrote
John Wilkes Booth over and over and hid the scraps
all about the house to magic him back whenever
his attentions strayed. Of course, we could infer
he was webbed in brother Johnny's "octopus
speculation," as he called his sinister business.

That winter while the South expired we entertained
so many visitors with masked faces and assorted
names, it was to the girl guests and me pure sport
I called the "Alias Game." A stag amid the dazzled
does, Pet could recite "The Driven Snow" to make
the very candles weep. We blushed and cooed
and fanned our cheeks, but behind the smile, a Randy
Dan was lurking. If Lincoln was "Hell's beast,"
we nodded agreement and brought him fresh tea
with just a tilt of brandy. Mother, not yet three

years a widow, was susceptible also, and said to me,
"Dear Anna, always remember these dark hours
when we struggled, but basked in his splendor."

Though that cursed era is at a close, poor Mother
is not forgotten. I was there at the end, having spent
my days weeping, endeavoring to see the president.
Johnson, I mean. She had been so ill with women
misery that her cell acquired an odor. The officers
had moved her to a gallery adjacent to the court,
where she could scarcely sit upright. She took
broth and clenched her olive rosary to rehearse
her steady devotions. At least she was not
ironed in full view. The prosecution's evidence?
Mere circumstance, the oaths of John Logan,
a drunk of substance, and her errant words. Even
the Yankee officials expected clemency. Seven
judges suggested life in prison, but his Excellency
said, "She kept the nest that hatched the egg." Later,
he claimed my petition never arrived. She sighed
to a priest on the scaffold, "Pray, do not let me fall."
General Hancock had posted riders across the capital
in case Johnson should send dispatches of reprieve.
Forgive the man? I curse him whenever I grieve.

Nights we sit beside the window as I recount it all
that my Clara will fathom her legacy. We prospered
in Prince George's County, our tavern a post office
and polling site, but father drank and misused us
until his heart failed. Mother, weary of pouring

thin lager and franking the mail, thought it better,
in light of extensive debts, to move to our house
on H Street, which I called "Horse Way" for the stable
and the stench of dung stamped into the cobbles.

Shadows came and went, some we knew to be spies,
my brother's "Confederate confederates," I jested,
so many harmless gossips and plotters. Code words
made them giddy, and the scheme they polished
over and over was to take Mr. Lincoln hostage
and exchange him for prisoners or a grand ransom.
Booth's hair was black as an officer's dress boot,
and Honora said he was her Crow. Every tenant
jumped at his mere suggestion. His manners were
so otherworldly, as if a character from some old
romance or tragedy. To think: he had uttered
doomed Romeo's anguished adieus and spoke
Henry's "Happy Few" speech before crowned heads,
and yet had discourse with rogues, that foreign man
we called Port Tobacco due to his twisted name
and the one who later drove the knife into Seward.
He was a brute, but since Mother doted on Booth,
we said nothing. No person with a heart would
imagine our mother a Lady Macbeth, hauling
"shooting irons"—as that snivel Weichmann said—
back and forth for felons. "Nemesis," the press
christened her. My beloved Mary was mild, pious,
a credit to her sex, but Pet's attention and wit—
right down to the swaggers and impromptu
dancing—distressed her balance, altered her
to frivolity under the gaselier's whispering jets.

True, we had held slaves and still kept servants,
but we thought it beneficent to harbor them thus.
Their toil was scarce more than ours, and yet
evil can serpent in, despite our best intentions.
Even here in Baltimore—where after four years
of plea and litigation we were able to inter
her plain box at Mount Olivet—we were not safe
from scorn and reprisal, and the churl's tomb
is scarce two miles from our home. Evil shadows
our tainted family, and once I met a gentleman
(self-proclaimed) who carried about in a sporran,
even to church, a splinter from those gallows!

I remember that dire afternoon, a magic lantern's
image burned in my brain: sun scorching, the wags
and vultures almost dizzy with revenge, a soldier
holding a black parasol to protect her, her modest
bombazine frock. Everything in march time,
a savage dignity. One moment I saw the pale flame
of her face, between her bonnet and the hood
of white cotton. An instant: she kissed the cross
and then was covered. I swooned to hear a senator
exclaim, "What, the woman, too?" I often wonder
if Booth was laughing from his grave. He gave
clues to implicate everyone he knew, but had they
seized him alive, so much would have clarified,
as I believe Mother, who had little malice to spend
her entire life, never guessed at his lethal ends.

For her it was, send someone to fetch a horse,
secure field glasses at the tavern, pass that jacket,

this note, a sisal rope. She obeyed and treasured
his smile, his scraps of lilting poems and a laugh—
how can I say?—to coax the very seraphs to humor.
They claim Captain Rath could only whisper the order
when the last chance of amnesty was forsaken.
Alas, two zouaves struck pylons at once, and four
black-clad forms dropped plumb. She perished
instantly. But what of justice? Even Nancy, when I
open the subject, weeps for poor Mary Surratt,
who played "Sweet Afton" softly on the piano
for her guests and could not keep a secret.

I hear the president's widow, who also found Pet
charming on the stage, went insane, her son
seeking to remove her to an asylum. Everyone
Booth touched was doomed to suffer. When William
wed me, he lost his position, and his practice
has never flourished, for word seeps out. At mass
daily we ask the Great Mystery if there is penance
to release us. No answer comes. Elusive clemency,
even for the innocent! So much is made of Mother
calling Booth an instrument in the Almighty's hands,
as she believed He works beyond our sapience.
That is how I must understand it, knowing her poise,
charity and grace. Even on that fatal Good Friday
she would have walked to church had not the rain
commenced in earnest. She wanted to light candles,
pray for her sons—Isaac in Texas, Johnny just gone
to Montreal on some mission. We saw him off
in his Garibaldi jacket and cap, a bashful paladin.

Did not Johnny's later acquittal on identical charges
certify her innocence? It was all Pet, his gaze
and persuasions, his tortured view of life. I once,
half in frolic, threatened the man with a kitchen knife,
should he bring my brother to mischief. He laughed,
and I was too charmed to sustain my suspicions.

What Mother did was open our home to displaced
persons who had known much sorrow and loss.
Perhaps she assisted Pet in minor smuggling—
camphor and quinine. What Christian would deny
a soldier his relief? Some women grew poppies
or knitted socks to promote the Cause and enjoy
status as heroines, while mother is universally reviled.
When one Union widow reported the ghost of Mary
Surratt by the docks on a foggy night, swarms
of reporters besieged our house, desperate to ask . . .
what? If she could not rest in peace? They shamed
our family, branded Mother a murderer, then
murdered her. When officer Clarvoe wrenched
her fragile wrists and clapped shackles upon them,
he said, "Madame, your star is but a cinder now.
May your house and its denizens suffer pain."
Our smiling villain brought us all to enduring harm,
and though the priests insist we trust in Providence,
who will care how such a nest of innocents
amid war's chaos can be so damned by charm?

One-Man Show

"a pitiless, dripping, carnivorous, slathered,
subhuman and antihuman beast mingling snake
and tiger; the unmentionable . . . a madman or
a snake—a lunatic . . . Booth."
　　　　　　　　　　　　—CARL SANDBURG

Before the Green Room mirror I touch up my mustache
with lamp black, as Booth did, and tighten the silk cravat,
artfully tousle my hair as he must have done for Brady's lens,
those poses we remember from high school textbooks:
*Booth the Assassin, Booth the Madman, The Insidious Villain
Booth*, all images instilled with generations of outrage.
Some evenings I impersonate his infamy in a college
auditorium, public library, or a Civil War scholar's parlor,
but tonight it's dinner theater, a festive venue, but peculiar.
They've already savored the buffet, as the viand chef
sliced the rare roast thin. They've dined to vintage
music and PowerPoint images of Ford's Theater. Cordials
soothe their palates. Silence rises as the house lights fall.
Soon, blue and red floods will cross over a center star.
I have a dagger, my derringer, and a box of props ready,
but in this half hour before illusion swings into motion,
I breathe deeply and rehearse my doubts. After all,
as Plato says, "A man's mask is apt to become his face."

"In dire times a new Brutus must rise," I whisper,
practicing my glare—or his—in the light-ringed mirror.
The tragic muse possesses me as I scowl and shiver.

I wanted independence and identity, to tread the boards
alone, a novelty, a tour de force. Thinking how Twain,
the Amherst Belle, and Will Rogers fueled others' success,
I yearned to play sad havoc to a packed house.
But Booth? my wife warned me. *A blatant racist, nutcase*
and assassin; what will people think? You expect applause?
At first I argued it was all audacity, surprise, and nerve. *Poe,*
she said, *was at least harmlessly creepy, despite the hints*
of incest, but Parmeleau holds a monopoly on that raven,
even resorting to cosmetic surgery to replicate his face.
I needed a trademark to market, a buzz, a "draw." Bierce,
she suggested, might be the ticket with his acid wit,
twisted epigrams, and misadventure south of the border.
An option, perhaps, but I wanted shock, hot language,
force, and Booth had the Bard's diction, plus a household
rife with rhetoric. Audiences crave boldness and blood,
so I give them Tybalt and Richard's discontented winter,
the famous "arms against a sea of troubles" from the Dane,
all filtered through conspiracy, ambition, tavern brandy
by the quart, his love of fast horses and skullduggery.
Add passages from the man's letters, reviews—both raves
and castigation. Besides, it's not all recitation. I aim
for catharsis and fill the stage with echoes and action.
My old fencing coach Beretti—God rest his nimble bones—
was infamous for parry and riposte in Italian fashion,
all rush and slash. A blade may prove the best metaphor
for Booth's mind. I work up a sweat in vintage tights
to banish my shadow with the cut and lunge of a Capulet:
fight scenes were always the rascal's forte, and he bore

many authentic wounds. When I resume his smoother
identity in a dandy's vest, tilted hat and riding crop,
my diamond stickpin and smirk cry out *clearly superior.*

And who among us, after all, is not intrigued by murder,
that *fleur de mal?* Everyone is curious, but I no longer
grant press interviews to Arts and Leisure editors,
all titillated but troubled, because when they inquire why
anyone would want to reenact a monster, even my
shrewdest answer rings false. It was fascination
at first: his lust for fame, the circuitry of a zealot,
and his crazed dismissal of any cost to the inner man.
He was id incarnate—voracious, reckless, yet intricate
and exact. Most people imagine him simple as a rabid dog,
but have you seen him rendered in Griffith's film *Lincoln*
by Ian Keith as a sawdust melodrama's rapscallion?
When he curses Old Abe for speaking of Negro freedom,
some walk-on identifies the firebrand as "Booth, the actor:
Can't act, but the ladies don't know it." So evil he's half
Dracula, half adder, all Caliban. But consider the innate
impulse to do something irrevocable? Not to preserve
slavery, of course, but something. If we paint him all
ebony and inhuman bile, we'll fail to grasp that ember
smoldering in the soul. The imp of misrule never sleeps,
and to fathom his dreams has long been my mission.
Risking the self to unravel a riddle: is that perverse?

Monday I received a registered letter inviting me to perform
in the hinterlands of Idaho for impressive remuneration.
I'd be flown first-class, no expense spared, to visit

"an independent community buried off the trodden path."
The brochure they enclosed for the Brethren of Rectitude
was rife with volatile rhetoric—"God's forgotten force,"
"mud people,""the Coming Conflict." It made me shiver.
They cite the Bible, the mark of Cain, and claim ambush is
politics by other means. "Who raises the venomed sword
must by the sword perish." Their pitch is pure Titus
Andronicus, but would they truly relish the chance to see a king
deposed in iambic pentameter? It's hardly my art of braiding
drama, history, and the dark heart they're eager to praise,

yet my antics can incite even the cretins to applause.
First, I always haul out a bloody scrap from *Macbeth*, crown
and mantle to impress any audience—"Life's but a walking
shadow . . . full of sound and fury." That sop. Then a sylvan
narrative: his boyhood Maryland, a troupe of kindred actors,
a fresh country's first First Family of the Stage, poetry,
and wisteria ubiquitous. The whole clan were vegetarians
and pacifists, but the children were shocked to learn
they were sown out of wedlock. Wilkes took it hardest
and strove to compensate, but imagine the mad father
roaming the woods with rum and slurred soliloquies!
Then I cut to the Crookback wanting a horse on Bosworth
Field—"Murder, stern murder, in the direst degree"—
followed by Booth's devoted letters to his fretting mother
who responded, "I am no Roman *mater*. I love my dears
before my country." She made him kneel and pledge never
to enlist in the army. He was no stock coward, and yet,
one has to wonder at the convenience of such filial piety.

Ah, the ready bell is ringing. Five minutes. The adrenalin
rush. Even in the Virginia swamp pursued by hounds
and shunned by the Old Dominion's citizens, the fugitive
thought he'd earn accolades from a grateful nation, believing
himself a patriot, a savior, the essential American Cousin.
Instead, he became the perfect agent of ruin.

For a time I considered expanding my repertoire: two acts,
loveable Lincoln first, followed by an addled Booth.
Unfortunately, the Emancipator, despite his humble words,
was majesty, wit, and stillness at the whirlwind's center,
sheer genius and easy for imposters to miss by a country mile.
At least it would seem more prudent and correct, and I'd
be protected from allegations of a sedition so sinister
and imprudent as to warrant my own swift arrest, indictment,
and exile, so uneasy are our nation's current powers.

One critic—this must have been enraging—wrote, "Booth
has skill and cunning, but in the end he does not astonish."
I make sure my last scene trumps that. In the doorway
of a torched tobacco barn he's fire-framed, crippled, defiant,
almost a phoenix. I save my most tortured expression
for that, then fade to black-out, the last word whispered
in darkness: "useless." I ask you, Is he our Lucifer,
or much less? I confess I have no shadow of an answer.
For a decade even to own his picture was a Federal offense,
yet years after his death travelers claimed the miscreant
managed a tourist hotel in Tunis and bought them drinks.
Perhaps that cowled imposter was the earliest actor
to earn attention and a living by declaring *ecce homo*.

Offstage and out of costume, I will no longer discuss
this twisted business. These days I spend my spare time
scripting a new project: Barnum, another rogue to hold me
in some strange thrall, but even when I'm in the throes
of composition, striving to wring humor from P. T.'s savvy,
the assassin comes back to me, spellbinding, light shot
through a prism with the doom syllable repeating—*Booth,
Booth, Booth.* Listen. The sinister anthem—it's "Dixie"—
is my cue to embody our bête noir and Gordian knot.
Blind anger and zeal: my soul or Booth's? Likely both.
Showtime. "This thing of darkness I do acknowledge."

Blood Harmony

Plantation of the Mad
BLUES FOR BUDDY BOLDEN

First photograph I ever saw of the East Louisiana
State Asylum was a postcard sent from Jackson
in September '09 by a guard, like it was a holiday

resort, an idea with all the charm of a cottonmouth
in the kiddie park. He was already there, you see,
after a third arrest for insanity. His wife and sister

said they couldn't stand his rage, and yeah, I came
to know Buddy right well. Lost my gig slabbing
plaster, so I got my cousin Bone to call in a favor.

I hired on as a ward watcher. By the end I'd seen
every inch of that sorrow farm. In the picture mailed
back to the Crescent City the antebellum façade

and Georgia columns said *Big Master*, the cupola
said *Money*, and sometimes he would climb up
and play on that nickel-flaking cornet they kept

locked away—"Make Me a Pallet," "The House Got
Ready," "Didn't He Ramble"—like the yard was full
of dancers thick as fleas. Me, I'm black as a spike

on the graveyard fence and ugly with some scars,
but Buddy was a beauty, a creamed coffee man,
dapper even in a crazy house homespun smock,

and when I'd come whispering to haul him down,
he'd say "Sebe"—that's my name, Sebe Brabham—
"don't you want to slow drag to 'Funky Butt Blues'?"

His signature. *Dementia praecox*, the chief doctor
wrote down, but Buddy could be plain straight,
and he blew that horn clear as death. You know

he was Kid Bolden before they crowned him King,
and he smoldered on the circuit, parks, and halls
like down on Perdido Street, the Flying Horses,

Mystic Babies, crewes like Ladies of Providence,
Knights of Pleasure. On day off, I'd slip down
to barrel houses in the swamp and get the skinny,

though even his running mates had half the stories
wrong. He smoked up a legend. Listen, he never
kept that scandal sheet *The Cricket*, and even his dear

sister was convinced he'd once been a barber.
Now, I have seen him eye a razor on shaving day,
but that look never meant to trim any man's hair.

Tending him in the asylum—you wouldn't buy
what I could tell you about inmates throwing
shit or ripping at their own eyes, gnashing teeth

like a junkyard bitch—well, I came to savvy no
soul truly knew Buddy Bolden at the center where
the demons hatched. But plaaay! And he turned

pure in the gazebo, riffing a solo—he would not
work with the madhouse band. Called them that,
he did—"Madhouse Band"—and laaaugh. Jesus!

I came later to hear Bechet, Armstrong, Kid
Ory, and they had finesse, embellishments
like pastries bought hot on the levee, but couldn't

a one Gabriel out like Buddy. Folks called him
High Note Man for a reason. He blew Judgment,
and I've seen him while ragging a hymn blast

the tuning slide across the room like a rocket.
Some say women did him in, a whole harem struck
hard by his star—that chippie Leda Chapman,

Hattie Oliver, some Emma, some Ella—and even
being sort of hitched to Nora didn't slow his note.
He liked their sashay, their candy voices, and flesh,

I reckon, but his breath was born for rowdy music,
smoke, cutting contests, and the Delta wildcat scream.
The ladies toted his bowler, his watch, his satchel,

but Big Whistle, who was his bank man, swore
no gal ever touched that brass horn. He carried
it like some will tote a baby or others hold a pistol,

the treasure. Red cigarettes and a taste for chicory
marked him as eccentric, a dog fox, and a dandy.
Outside, he loved funerals and cockfights equal,

and the wags say he was all piss and whiskey.
One night my first year—moon full, air musky—
he freed a trumpet from the band's locker. Buddy

was meant to be locked in, sure: I turned the key,
but strange things pass for normal in such a place.
Buddy slipped to the garden—June, the world rife

with magnolia and summer sumac rampant. He spit
in that kiss piece and woke everybody like End
Time. Joseph in the morgue said a corpse sat up.

I jumped off my bench like a man stuck in the belly.
Mostly, though, he just drifted quiet, doing what
the doctors called crazy, following a ritual of touch

and stroke—door frame, chair arm, a special spot
on the ward floor, all the while working a scuffle
slide like a man dancing inside. Lightning, I always

thought, was flashing red in his mind. He brought
a whole Fat Tuesday float of ghosts for company,
and he'd say names over and over, you know—

Willie Cornish, John P. Robichaux, Butterfoot
and Bang Zang, Alcibiades Jeanjacques—I expect
you've met a few, down to Willis Spillis, Mumford,

the boys from the Silver Leaf, Baptiste Delisle.
He'd rave till we strapped him in the cold pack.
Poor bastard. Crazy ain't anybody's holiday.

It's likely he was haunted, but he had no hanker
to get back to the city. I asked, and even on those
ice cream days when he'd bear to speak: no word

on that matter. One day he told me the vanilla
in Jackson was better than shrimp. He winked:
"Know what I mean? The pink shrimp." Honest!

When his orchestra of ghosts thiefed in, no solid
man could claim his attention, and he spoke
often in bird to the local birds or passing pelicans

and gulls. They'd strap him up again whenever
he'd start tearing at his shirt. Yeah, it's true he'd
up and babble like one of the others. But I guess

I loved him a little, the way he'd strut and funk-step
when he wasn't sick or bedeviled. I was never
tempted to preach him Jesus, a sport like that,

a man with style and a genius lip. That smile
would cut you at the knees, but he played it hot
with the brass, red sauce, and peppered oysters,

no mercy, hardcore, jazzy with the fury of a man
driving a horse to Hell, B flat, flat out, making
the sound fresh by sheer scream. They say

his mother wept on visits at first, and he'd calm
and promenade her. She brought him peaches,
but by the end, I couldn't get lick sense from him,

just gobble-gabble, bobbing like a walking crow,
his color gone ashy, drab skin hanging on him
like wattles. And I never could quite suss out—

so don't get me started—the big mystery, why life
hurt him so, why he fell from King Bolden
to pure misery. I could rattle on about how maybe

the music in his mind was cold and running wild
in a circle he couldn't shake out, but that would be
a guess. Don't get me started. They say he broke

his cherry, I mean gigged out for public hearing,
down on Liberty Street and Perdido, that word
which might could whisper why we'll never

have an answer, as *perdido* still means *lost*.

NOTE: Buddy Bolden (1877–1931) was one of the first great
New Orleans cornet players and served as an early inspiration
to Louis Armstrong. A natural-born whirlwind, he had a brief
and mercurial career as a musician and was institutionalized in
the asylum in Jackson, Louisiana, before he reached thirty.
Although no recordings and few documents about him sur-
vive, all the rumors and legends are in accord: he played hot.

Mandolin

Dog days, flat heat, the sky tight
as a Holiness tambourine. I am walking the road
gouged out to make way for Saddle Ridge Acres
and mourning the slaughter of timber,
but someone down the bulldozed slope
is striking true notes like fireflies in the August air.

For troubadours of the courtly age
this sound was a lute, a pear-shaped, four-stringed gourd
to set the mood for chivalry and wit,
but it picked up a set of shadow strings
and outlived vaudeville irony,
the sweet tremolo of parlor play,
and ragtime just jaunty enough for cakewalks,

till what I hear is the amplified flatback
Orville Gibson gave it, an ebony bridge
with bronze strings too taut to jump the nut,
and this musician playing somewhere, I'm guessing,
down by Buckle Creek, near the narrows
where water rills quick and clear,

is tuning to the seven-year insects
resuming their shivaree in the evergreens,

not quite the holy call and response,
but something secular and just as desperate.

It's a miniature instrument for delicate fingers
strong enough to shiver a fret,
and in this heat I drink it in like water
from a mint spring as I remember
how young Ricky Skaggs, already
a picking prodigy and keen to blend gospel
with his old-time riffs, asked Bill Monroe
the secret to becoming a great player
of the bluegrass mandolin,
and the master looked hard into the sky's mystery
and back at the plectrum of tortoiseshell
shaped like a deer tick in his fingers
before he answered the boy:
"Son," he said, "you got to whip it like a mule."

And that is the fiery melody I hear
over the cicadas' amber serenade
of breakdown, blues licks, and frantic reel.
Even on this worksite the county fathers call
progress, I bow to the enduring thirst for melody

and thank a lonesome picker, as the full moon
round as a cat-skin banjo sails
over the remnant saw-toothed pines.
For hopeful good measure and the ghost of harmony,
I cut a shuffle step, kick my heels, and twirl
in the rusted dust on the margin
of this sleeping, mongrel world.

The Carter Scratch

What solitude and simmer gave birth
to this sweet mix, one country woman
strumming a duet, melody running
the bass but the high strings
thumb-brushed for back-up rhythm?
It's a mystery how her touch
contrived what's called the Carter Scratch.
Maybe it was mischief in her black guitar.
Maybe the Clinch Mountains are to blame.

Her fingers were deft but leathered
from scraping in the hardscrabble earth
to snatch choke weeds from the bean vines
and strong as claws from plucking hens
or shucking the stubborn corn.
She'd heard the river chord fast over rapids
and smooth at the soothing ford,

so Maybelle rocked in the dark parlor
to raise the cadence—"The Storms
Are on the Ocean," "Bury Me Under
the Weeping Willow." Stitch by stitch,
she improvised an outlaw style, and after
the Bristol Sessions the whisper
talk in Nashville was, "These ridgers
can really pick." She played like sisters

and kept her Gibson warm in the kitchen.
One hand's nails were sharp as talons.
To keep her spirit busy, she'd sing
and hum and whistle—hymns of the heart,
skimp and yearn of the stricken flesh.
She'd fret and frail the strings to bliss,
while coffee boiled and corncakes frizzled.
Maybelle called herself a "Nickelsville hick"
and often played at being rapt and simple
to keep the curious at a distance,
as her nimble hands gave country music
its intricate, quintessential lick.

Strange Fruit, 1939

June and rumor and Georgia dew.
Hattie McDaniel was bustling Mammy
at the Loews Grand in downtown Atlanta
when Billie Holiday took up
the jazzy anthem of blood on the leaf,
blood at the root,

and my granddaddy loved
the gardenia scent of the torch singer's voice
etched into the Commodore LP disk
with his bourbon and branch,
though he never listened hard to the words.

His old Colt with the misfire hammer
was losing nickel plate in the roll-top desk
as he drank to excess—
whiskey the color of honey—
and kept vigil—I'm divining this—
with the Bible or his Tuscan fiddle

eager for the midnight phone to ring
and shake its cradle. The story is still
a puzzle—a white waitress at the Wagon Wheel
heard a hot laugh and an off-key snicker,
a spark on spilled gasoline.

In the shadow of the capitol's
gold dome, Miss McDaniel's

face was a dark moon sweating. "Chile,"
she said, "you behave." Any chance
of a pastoral died as the edge of a gardenia
corsage wilted and the men's
club met to cast their secret votes.

Sisal rope coiled like a snake
in a Chevrolet's boot. An evil orchard,
strange fruit. "Sepien songstress"
a pundit called Holiday. The full moon
was a quivering cymbal. The crowd
at the Roxy was filing out,
still shocked by Rhett's staircase
"I don't give a damn."

What dust skirled on the road to Jackson?
What corrupt brotherhood dispersed
in the fog of dawn? The peaches
were bleeding, cigarette ash
smoldered, and the savage sun
came up over Macon with a scream.

Rise an octave, skid to a whisper,
a grim tremolo, then insinuation,
lament, pianissimo, a bitter crop.
A summer fever. Your neck hair
will stiffen like hackles,

and what can I do but sip my tepid Coke
and try to say *No* with every word

or silence I dare remember,
write this family testament
soft as a moth, black ink gliding across—
I will save myself if I can—
this bond stationery's
bone-white killing field.

Johnny Shines' Last Edict
on the Taproot of Delta Blues

(AT THE END ZONE LOUNGE, APRIL 1990)

I stock no faith to the myth that Robert Johnson
took a crossroads rendezvous with your Devil,
Papa Legba, or Tush Hog hisself to sell his soul
at midnight for blue music. I scoff it, son.

That boy strummed on the diddley bow, two wires
nailed to shed planks. He'd pluck a two-note baritone—
doom-doom, doom-doom. Next he started mouth harp,
then slide guitar. White boys want to sleuth it:

how he got so good so quick. One bad eye, sure,
but nothing wrong with Robert's ears. He drink up
every lick he ever hear. His chops was wind and rain,
a screen door slap. He got the magic prowess

like lightning. I never seen him practice once.
Rust spots where somebody touch magnolia flower
showed him moods. Glean skills from rills a-whisper
through loose levee sacks. Fetched them riffs from bottle

clank and the bedspring sag. Reaped them from moan
love and trains. Good looking, Lord, washed in charm,
but he was cunt-struck, mad for women, just not mean,
like the record jackets claim. Ask Ginny Tarvis,

Vergie Mae Smith, sleek Caletta Craft. Only Queen
Elizabeth ever say he hand-slapped her. Friend Robert
used women like some men use a hotel room—
lie down hard, then move on. Listen at "Cross Road

Blues," "Hell Hound on My Trail," "Dust My Broom."
He knew hurt, you right, but what mortal don't,
gnawing at the wishbone? He was a walkin musician,
same as the rest, got the sorrows and the rapture,

got six strings to build his fence. The high pitch
and the low, bottle neck, and fingers his only
mojo. Stomp a foot, sing in that moaning minor
rasp. Moon behind a cloud? That was him.

First leaf to yellow and walk the wind? Yeah, him.
Son House showed him up-stroke and counter
the point, but playing jooks or grab-alls, he fell deep
into his own self till that gig in Three Forks

every savvy picker now knows: messed with a wench
whose man poured the hooch. You know "passagreen"?
They use it as a douche. No hoodoo, just poison
in the rye. Yeah, he heard that scalded hell hound

howling down the end. Gaunt, wrong-eyed, on all-fours
barking like a cur, he died with a Monkey Ward
guitar across the room, a not-human shadow stain
on the wall I can't explain. You say it's Satan,

that's maybe your personal curse, but brother,
he was the best, the sap root. Touch him, was a heat.
But no spite, conscience clean as a choir girl's purse.
They put him in the ground at Zion Church.

Time to get busy now. Can't do no worse than worst.
We walk the harmony slow to echo like his ghost.
This Cajun here my complice called Kent Duchain.
For a white boy, I promise he can get good lost.

Here come a blood blues Robert called his "Terraplane."
In the end, we all just freight on the westbound train.

Hohner

Who thought it up, this reservoir
of sorrow, tang of chrome, taste of cedar?

I first learned to spit and whisper
through a one-octave mini-twitter

from a Cracker Jacks box. *Blow, harder,*
Freddie said, then showed me. I'd shutter

when high notes went sharp and compare
low riffs that meant slow surrender

to a lonely life's most deadly measures.
I learned my best licks on a battered Hohner

my uncle saved from his navy years.
And nights on the slow Flint River's shore

I'd practice with trill and trains, pure dolor
and Fanny Crosby's holy sweet forevers.

A solo act, outcast and night walker,
I'd set out at a fast canter to inspire

myself. I'd cup my palm for a mute or
give all my breath to "Fair and Tender

Ladies,""Shenandoah,""Wayfaring Stranger,"
but it was hard love blues I'll always remember

as the natural weather for the raspy fervor
of a mouth harp's razor edge, that stridor

and chromatic keen under the embouchure
uttered only as kiss and spitfire

by woman wailing for her demon lover,
all caterwaul, moan, and broken-soul-shiver.

The Sacred Sound of the Dove

I have come back from the far field
with my bloody sack full of flutterless birds
knocked from the sky and riddled with pellets,
the last flash of sunset in their underfeathers,

and I have spent hours plucking and gutting
for the taste of a meager but wilder meat
and known the flavor of brass
across the cracked tooth, and I will not say

I failed to understand that the dove is chosen,
that he was Noah's blessed messenger
and God's envoy of annunciation,
for his reticent humble cooing is the sound

of grace amazing, which did not save me—
striding beyond the peach orchard
and the empty gestures of our single pecan tree—
from the heart's high singing at the thought

of blood, even as a southerly covey passing over
veered low and slowed to study me.
I could see their wings glittering,
and sometimes I still feel the twin triggers

of the Browning tickling my finger
and believe the blued barrels could blast

across the sky a song of my power
and pleasure, which is why I can still shiver

when a country preacher, inviting the choir
to stir us all from lust and lethargy,
turns his blazing face to heaven to say,
"Not even the mockingbird on his black limb

can mimic the lament of the blessed dove."

Gypsy Fiddle

How it came to my wife's grandmother
I can't guess, but the violin locked
in our hall closet is a spell

hewn in evergreen and ebony,
Alpine maple, an hourglass sawed, whittled,
and assembled in some lamp-lit forest camp

with mother-of-pearl chips inlaid
to shape a wildflower. The rough-cut f-holes
curve like serpents on the belly,

while nicks and scars in the varnish
almost tell the secret history
of Cain's progeny, the lost tribe vagrant

on a moonlit mountain road. The music
knew how to say they suffered.
Spun sheep gut anointed with oil of the olive

draws tight and ready for the arpeggios
of an open fire, the cart wheel, the cards, and evil
eye. Because they were shunned, I'm reluctant

to touch it, to let my fingerprints mar
its sheen, but the color's irresistible,
all amber lac and madder, first light

of a haunted dawn. It can chuckle like a hen,
mimic rain or lure the train sound
from a distant ravine. Owl screech

in the aftermath of thievery is its specialty,
but the broken heart is always
underscoring the chord structure.

It can freshet, shirr, and flurry,
pattern like a spider and conjure a silk shawl,
black with red tassels, or a knife

under the jerkin, and I'm actually happy,
or nearly, that my wife has little time
to work its magic, to grip its edge

between chin and shoulder and show her
virtuosity. Such magic is equally curse
and cure, the whisper legends tell us

must be the Devil's lure: piercing pitch,
crescendo, the slip from gigue to minuet,
the song of stars dying in the sky.

What it says is how to survive misery,
the wake after cruel death, the promise
in passion's amulets. It's dangerous

for anyone to listen to such a device
rent, shaved, riven, and joined again
by sleight-of-hand, the art of hiding mystery,

the kind of man who could make a tree speak
of everything from joy to grief
the way the Sabine goddess Vitula

taught the ancients to mesmerize any
villager: use a fiddle whose supple bow
is strung with horse hair and kin to a whip.

Sometimes, passing by
the closet door, I fancy I can hear scraps
of cant, caravan springs, a jangle

that is not hangers colliding, a rustle
something other than our winter clothes feeling
wanderlust. That's when I ask my wife

to see to her instrument's security,
before my feet answer with a manic dancing
that is melancholy and frenzy,

for not even the hardshell case and a pair
of chrome locks snapped with the blessing
of a priest in good standing

can arrest such highstrung sylvan witchery,
the vernacular voltage that will never
leave a dazed man alone.

Bury Me Under the Weeping Willow

Sara Carter's Roebuck autoharp was never
strung with baling wire nor carved
from the heart of a gallows tree,
and the flower hole cut in the cherry soundboard
was not the dark blossom offered at any grave,
but her eerie tremolo on laments
and valley ballads, Galilee Gospel,
or a freight train's lonesome moan
always carried that quavering keen,
like a pain from the rim of the world.

She'd hold the instrument high and strum
like soothing an ailing child till she found
an owl's healing calls in the chord bars,
sassafras tea and copperhead tonic,
anything close by to summon good luck,
but she could also blend her notes
like someone knotting a noose.
People said her troubled voice could mourn
or scorch a wound or quench a thirst.

When Pleasant wed her she was just sixteen
and already lonely as a wandering ghost,
with a voice so private it could shave ice.
She smothered in the bosom of family and faith,
the frozen air of her Clinch Mountain home,

but learned the moody melodies
of a straying tongue and tossed her hair,
black-bright as a seam of number nine coal.

The dovetailed sound of clinging kin
known in music circles as "blood harmony"
took the country market by storm.
These hillbillies, one critic wrote, *are blessed,*
but things went wrong, then worse and worst.
Their burdened accent and ghostly yodel
were torn by blue eyes of a cousin named Coy.

Some say God will pardon and forgive and mend,
but in the later sessions you can always hear
a stray ember burning through the hymns,
the pitch flickering even in "Sunny Side."
Hard times, hard love, she was never the same.

When she passed, her shroud was fine
as courting lace, and somebody tossed in rose
petals straight from a forlorn song.
Please, Jesus, can we get an amen?
Can music ever promise the end of pain?

Beyond the brow of the graveyard's mountain
a fog the woodsmoke color of a tarnished mirror
snagged on the spruces of Crow Crest Peak
and on wraithy voices only the bereft can hear
sent its winter misery of wildwood rain.

Summertime

ONE OF THESE MORNINGS,
YOU'RE GONNA RISE UP SINGING . . .

First of June, gate to the season of parch and swelter,
it's the fabled year of the Millennium
and the doctor hasn't yet said *cancer,*
so I take down the dreadnaught Martin
and make sure the mouse I shook from the soundbox
last winter to my own blinking horror
has found another harbor. What I want, while a green
hornet plays his light-starved rhythm
against the double-glazed pane, is the only Gershwin
my hands have mastered. It's "Summertime,"
the lullaby I play as joyful lament,
shadowed with flamenco chords I stole
from Segovia and a whitewater rubato run with tremolo
Doc Watson showed me on a video.

I am all keen ears and nostalgia's hum,
for such sweet spruce with rosewood tunes easy,
even with last year's stretched and sweaty strings.
At ease, alone, I twiddle and strum, allegro, moderato.
I don't yet know that a daily blaze of radiation
will soon twist my hearing and the scalpel
will alter my voice and the mortal channel
where I hold notes to change and savor them,
that chemo will maim the taste of my favorite words.

"And the living is easy," shivers down my labored
tenor to make DuBose Heyward's lyrics quake
and simmer. The flat light of evening sweetens
on the wood's patina. It's my last time
to hear it so pure, though I don't know it yet,
the catfish jumping, the high lowland cotton,
the lyric embrace of the torturous season
that will christen a year of prayers and medicine.

The tortoiseshell pick leads my breath down a key
to echo "spread your wings and take to the sky"—
a little Lou Rawls, a touch of Iggy Pop,
but nothing of the reckless distress flashed by Janis.
It is a moment of almost-innocence,
hands and vocal apparatus bridging the abyss
between the pastoral repose of home and final asylum.
Against all instinct, I have to call it *bliss*,
the self-dazzled spell of homemade beauty,
though as always I take the guitar by the neck
and strangle it against the languor of the chords,

as if already knowing how even mercy
is ruthless, how reprieve is sure to wound and no melody
ever etched in tablature can make the living easy
or suffering hush or a minor key promise good news.
Suddenly, the Audubon clock's midnight owl
behind me hoots the hour in remarkable harmony,
and looking out, I discover, against all probability,
I have somehow summoned the moon.

NOTE

I am indebted to the authors of the following books, which I have steeped in at various times during the creation of this collection:

American Brutus: John Wilkes Booth and the Lincoln Conspiracies by Michael Kauffman (Random House, 2004).

American Gothic: The Story of America's Legendary Theatrical Family—Junius, Edwin, and John Wilkes Booth by Gene Smith (Simon and Schuster, 1992).

American Ornithology by Alexander Wilson (Bradford & Inskeep, 1814).

American Sphinx: The Character of Thomas Jefferson by Joseph J. Ellis (Vintage, 1998).

Bluegrass: A History by Neil Rosenberg (Illinois, 1985).

Bluegrass Breakdown: The Making of the Old Southern Sound by Robert Cantwell (Illinois, 1984).

The Escape and Capture of John Wilkes Booth by Edward Steers Jr. (Thomas, 1983).

The Fruits and Trees of Monticello: Thomas Jefferson and the Origins of American Horticulture by Peter J. Hatch (Virginia, 1998).

The Grail Bird: Hot on the Trail of the Ivory-Billed Woodpecker by Tim Gallagher (Houghton Mifflin, 2005).

Hope Is the Thing with Feathers: A Personal Chronicle of Vanished Birds by Christopher Cokinos (Tarcher/Putnam, 2000).

In Search of Buddy Bolden, First Man of Jazz by Donald Marquis (LSU, 1978, 2005).

Lust for Fame: The Stage Career of John Wilkes Booth by Gordon Samples (McFarland, 1982).

"Right or Wrong, God Judge Me": The Writings of John Wilkes Booth, edited by John Rhodehamel and Louise Taper (Illinois, 1997).

Robert Johnson, Lost and Found by Barry Lee Pearson and Bill McCulloch (Illinois, 2003).

ABOUT THE AUTHOR

R. T. SMITH is the author of several books of poems, including *Messenger*, *Brightwood*, and *The Hollow Log Lounge*. His collections of short stories are *Faith* and *Uke Rivers Delivers*, and he edited (along with his wife, Sarah Kennedy) *Common Wealth: Contemporary Virginia Poets*. Smith has received fellowships in poetry and fiction from the Virginia Commission for the Arts, the Alabama State Council for the Arts and the NEA. His work has appeared in *The Atlantic Monthly*, *Virginia Quarterly Review*, *Southern Review*, *Georgia Review*, *The Sewanee Review*, and other journals. A former Alumni Writer-in-Residence at Auburn University, he has been since 1995 the editor of *Shenandoah: The Washington and Lee University Review* and currently lives in Rockbridge County, Virginia. His website is rtsmith.org.